A Jar of Summer

And Other Poems

A Jar of Summer

Barbara Peckham

AuthorHouse™
1663 Liberty Drive
Bloomington, IN 47403
www.authorhouse.com
Phone: 1-800-839-8640

Published by AuthorHouse   04/27/2013

ISBN: 978-1-4817-4401-0 (sc)
ISBN: 978-1-4817-4402-7 (e)

Library of Congress Control Number: 2013907400

Contents

Dedication

In memory of my mother,
Marguerite Pope,
who taught me to love poetry
and whose poems I still treasure.

Preface

I credit my mother with my great love of words. From the time I was small, she always read to me, especially poetry. As I grew older I started writing my own stories and poems. I became editor of my high school newspaper. Later in life, I looked for jobs in the writing field and became Society and Woman's Page Editor of the New Haven, Connecticut *Journal Courier*. For some years I wrote radio and television commercials for an Albany, New York advertising agency, and later I became an English teacher. Although I have had individual pieces published, I have never attempted a book! When I came to live on Martha's Vineyard in 2001, I found inspiration in everything around me, and a number of years ago I joined the Oak Bluffs Public Library Writing Group.

I owe a huge debt of gratitude to the members of that group, particularly the Rev. Judy Campbell, Peggy McGrath, Charles Blank, Stephanie Michalczyk, Kay Mayhew, Laurel Chapman, Joyce Lockhart, Debbie Dean, and Madhu Lassiter, for their criticism and encouragement. So many other friends have given me encouragement and advice that it would be impossible to name them. However, I need to mention a few who, along with the writing group, have given me the impetus to publish this book. Susan and Bob Stevenson and Bess and Bob Stone, thank you. Without your gentle prodding, I might never have gotten this far!

And of course, it goes without saying that my family has been more than enthusiastic and, especially my three children, who all also write poetry! Thank you, also, to my patient husband, Douglas, to whom I am indebted for illustrations in the book.

WINTER

A Jar of Summer

Snow lies thick on the yard
Outside my window.
I lift the jar from the shelf
And carry it to my breakfast table.
Sunlight glows purple through the glass.
I pry open the lid.
And the winey aroma
Fills my soul with summer.

I see the grass by the fence.
The air is heavy with
The musky smell of wild grapes
That hang in beckoning clusters
From vines among the trees.
I clamber over the fence,
My hip complaining
About that last leg over!

I scramble among the grasses –
Never mind the thorny creepers
Clutching at my legs and clothes –
And load my bag with purple jewels.
The jam kettle waits,
And I hurry home to fill
The neighborhood with the
Thick, sweet aroma of cooking grapes.

This little jar of jam I open
At my winter breakfast table
Holds all the memories of summer.
I close my eyes and let
The tart-sweet taste
Fill my all my senses with
The sun and smells and tastes
Of summer past and summer yet to come.

Winter Dance

I heard the singing of the stars
In a deep blue winter night.
I heard the hum of the universe,
And it filled me with delight.

I rode on a blazing comet far
Across an electric sky
Beneath a sliver of silver moon
Shivering there on high.

I watched as the rosy, golden dawn
Painted the eastern sea,
And I sang to the sun of stars and moon
That danced the night with me!

They Only Sleep

Beneath a quilt of leaden sky,
By the crumpled sheet of sea,
The frozen bushes huddle low,
Stiff, bare and stark in winter garb
Of rusts and browns and blacks,
Under threadbare blankets of snow.

A heatless sun shines pale
Upon their hibernating forms.
The bitter winds and biting cold
Disturb them not at all,
As they sleep there, dreamless,
In deepest winter's hold.

They will nothing know
Until a brighter, warmer day
Brings forth an urge for sap to run,
And they awake to breathe
A kinder air, don green again,
And dance in leafy fun!

First Snow

The sky hung low and cold
And gray all morning.
Then the snow began,
Softly, just a whisper at first,
Now heavier and faster,
Whipped by the wind.
It doesn't really fall,
Unless falling can
Be construed to mean
Going sideways and in circles!

Soft wet flakes land thickly
On hats, mufflers, coats,
Mittens and boots that are
Hurrying up the street,
Looking like bundles
Of walking clothes
With no people inside!
Muffled by the snow, no sounds
Except the wind soughing and
Snow sh-sh-shing in the twilight.

Outside the town, drifts form
Like rumpled quilts,
Shifting and moving as if
Something underneath is
Trying to get more comfortable.
The snow piles up on fences,
Trees and walks. I make some tea.
Time enough tomorrow to shovel.
Andy, why are you barking?
Oh, no! You have to go OUT?

Beach in Winter

Sleet hoar-frosts the dunes,
Icing starched brown grass,
Which crackles underfoot
Like shards of broken glass.

And far off, toward the sea,
The bleak dunes stretch away
To the jetty and beyond
Beneath a canopy of gray.

No fields of gay umbrellas
Are blooming here and there.
No children's shouts and laughter
Infuse a summer's air.

Instead, the dismal waves
Are crashing on the sand.
The wind is blowing sideways,
And I can hardly stand.

Soon winter's hold will break
And spring be on the way.
For above the gray is sun
To bring that warmer day!

Snow on Pennacook Park

Snow whirls past my window,
Topping fence posts
In the park to give them
Furry, tilted caps.
The posts and trunks
Of trees are dressed
In sparkling robes of white,
And roads wear cotton wraps

Inside my house,
I watch the drifting snow,
Lap robe tucked around,
And slippers on my feet.
A china mug of cocoa
Warms my hands and
Wafts a chocolaty steam
That makes my life complete.

The wind can snarl
And try to rip the
Shingles from the roof,
And yet I fear no storm.
While winter wreaks its
Worst outside, here I,
With kitten on my lap,
Sit comfy, loved, and warm!

January Thaw

I sit on the worn, wooden bench
High above Sunset Lake.
My dog lies at my feet, dozing
After his leisurely morning walk.
The air is chill, but the sun feels
Warm and soft against my face.
A gentle breeze ruffles the grass –
No bitter, icy wind today!

A rime edges a silver shimmer of ice
On the eastern half of the lake,
Leaving the rest a pale, diluted blue,
Reflecting the milky sky.
The quiet touches me. I do not hear
The Matchbox cars that race
Along the wet, black road
Between the harbor and the lake.

No waves slapping against the bulkhead,
No boats in this time of winter waiting –
Only mooring stakes crazily tilted.
I look down on the Monopoly houses
In their festive, colored dress
And store this time of utter peace
In the album of my mind
For the later years to come.

Calendar

I wonder almost every time
When I get out of bed,
What is it I should do today?
And so, to clear my head,
I check the little dated squares
Of the calendar on my wall.
Is it Monday or a Tuesday?
Why can I not recall?
For now that I'm retired
And have so much more time
Why do the days go by so fast?
It really seems a crime!

My friends who live off-island
Will often question me.
"Whatever do you DO there
All winter near the sea?"
I say I have the church choir,
And Solar Greenhouse bunch,

Several more committees,
And friends to meet for lunch.
There's League of Women Voters,
And non-profits by the zillion.
There are movies, parties, concerts,
Things number in the millions!

I love the peace and quiet
Of the Vineyard's vacant shores
To wander, seeking beach glass
Without the thronging hordes!
It only takes me minutes
To drive to Vineyard Haven!
Without Five Corners' traffic,
Just think what gas I'm saving!
So I'm busy, yes, but only
On MY terms, not a rut!
And my calendar's what helps me
To remember which is what!

Snow Robins

Today I saw two robins –
They must have lost their way.
It's only January and
Months and months 'til May.

They pecked along the snowbanks
As chipper as could be.
Don't they know the temperature's
Just barely thirty-three?

I wonder if they're omens
To say warm days are near
Or if they just came early
To bring some winter cheer!

It really doesn't matter
'Cause I can't do a thing
To shorten up this winter
Or hurry up the spring!

I'll just enjoy the robins
As they're hopping in the snow
And hope that they are privy
To something I don't know!!

Weather Isn't Life!

I'm getting tired of sleet and snow.
Whenever will this season go?
My patience almost is undone!
It seems' if spring will never come.

The winds that blow are chilling me,
And there's no green that I can see!
The roads still have some patchy ice,
And the dirty snow banks don't look nice,

But, nasty as the day may be,
This much I know with certainty –
The days are getting longer now,
And spring's about to take a bow.

I smell a difference in the air,
And, although the trees are bare,
A sense of expectation flowers –
March gives way to April showers.

Once more I hear the basketballs
Bouncing on the streets and walls.
More birds are singing every day.
I KNOW that warmth is on the way!

But wait! Don't wish my life away!
Enjoy and taste it, come what may!
For sweet or bitter be the flavor,
Each fleeting moment I must savor!

SPRING

The Undecided Month

In March the weather can't decide
Just what it wants to do!
First icy winds will freeze our bones,
Then sun will warm us through

And make us cast our cares aside
And watch for bursting buds,
Or leave our boots at home and slosh
Through puddles filled with mud.

One day it's kites and sweaters,
The next the snowflakes fly.
But every day grows longer now.
Spring signs are all nearby.

A robin sings, skateboards appear,
And, through the melting snows,
Right there, in all its glory,
A purple crocus glows.

Spring Pickup

Although the trees are nearly bare
I know that spring is everywhere,
For crocuses and small green shoots
Are pushing through and growing roots.
And through the last of winter's snow
I catch a glimpse of... what? Oh, no!

I see what's left of winter's trash –
Tin cans and papers – what a stash
Of cellophane, six-packs, and bags,
Some plastic, "nips," dog poop and rags!
Now how can humans be so crass
As to spoil the spring – alas!

But then I spy some walkers who
Hike the roadsides, looking, too!
They come prepared with sack and box
And pick up junk, fish line, and socks
Until the countryside is clean.
At last spring's beauty can be seen!

Cinquains

SELF-PORTRAIT

I see
Green shoots poking
Through the frozen brown ground.
They are struggling to find the sun,
Like me!

HOPE

Indoor
Green plants brighten
Dreary light coming through
My windows, dirtied by the snow
And rain.

FRESH BREAD

The yeast
Smell rises from
The bread I made today,
Baking and browning in the oven.
Oh, joy!

Haiku

SPRING

The sun is shining
And the birds sing cheerily.
What a lovely day!

MARCH CHRISTMAS

My Christmas cactus
Blossoms on St. Patrick's Day!
Are we both confused?

EQUATION

Sorrow bends my spirit
And weighs down my heart in pain.
Where is the answer?

Lost – One Spring

Where could it be?
I know last Sunday
Was supposed to be the
First day of spring, but
Uninvited, in its place, came
Rain and stinging sleet,
Snow, and a bitter,
Gusty north wind gale.

The tiny new crocuses
Huddle for warmth
In little purple clumps.
Half-frozen, the daffodils
Hang their golden
Trumpet heads in misery!
Forsythia, barely yellow,
Shivers in the whipping wind.

The green-black harbor sea
Is thick with choppy waves
And whitecaps, slapping
Up against the piers and pilings.
Rain pelts the water, and
The few boats left at dock
Rock up and down, back
And forth, like fairway rides.

So then, where IS spring –
That gentle in-between season
For which we wait so long?
Could it be just an illusion?
Will we be watching and
Waiting and then, surprise!
Wake up one day to find
That summer's come?

Ode to Spring

Welcome spring! Its lightness like a feather
That soothes our winter-blasted, frosted souls
With gentle rains and soft and balmy weather
That lifts our spirits up from murky shoals
Of icy sleet and snow and long dark days!
A crowd of singing birds once more appears
To flutter 'round the feeder and the trees.
We revel in sun's rays
And welcome lilacs, peonies with tears
Of joy, while apple blossoms buzz with bees.

Our privilege to view the change of seasons
Occurring right before our very eyes,
And maybe showing everyone the reasons
Why spring's the time of year that we most prize.
We rake the leaves and there, below, are shoots
Of tender green that reach up for the sun
And promise vibrant hosts of fragrant blooms
And later summer's fruits,
To please the eye of passersby and stun
My friends with sweet bouquets to grace their rooms.

I offer up my thanks and greet the spring,
The rains that patter gently on the grass,
That touch my face with soft, caressing cling
And make lovers of a young lad and his lass,
The pale green new-born buds of waking trees
Against the watercolor palette of the sky,
Children's laughter once more in the air
 Soaring on the breeze
That brushes by as gently as a sigh.
So here's to spring! That season ever fair!

Spring Parade

I stepped outside this morning
Into spring!
A softness in the breeze that
That barely touched my skin
Held misty warmth
And whispered in my ear:
"Come walk with me."
As I walked, senses heightened,
I marveled at the
Passing spring parade!
Tiny grape hyacinths in purple uniforms
Stood stiffly at attention
All along the road.
Behind them, stately
Ladies – tulips and daffodils –
Decked out in rainbow colors,
On carpets of pink phlox,
Were dancing to the
Music of the breeze!
And then I saw
Whole floats of trees
Reaching out their arms
To bless their audience,
Showering their petals
On pale green grass, not yet mown,
Where tiny birds hid
And hopped and pecked
Among the blossoms.
Bees buzzed, half-drunk with the
Heavy perfume of
Apple blossoms, mock orange.
I caught my breath in awe and
Marvelled at this spring parade,
Not remotely rivaled
By its man-made counterpart!

A Space of Time My Own

Tiny new, soft green leaves,
Yet full of baby wrinkles
And winter sleep,
Uncurl and stretch,
Clinging to mother branches,
Basking in the unaccustomed
Long-awaited,
Sun-filled warmth.

Bird conversations
Fill the soft-stirred air.
Returning wanderers
Greet one another.
"Hello again! How was
Venezuela this year?
Who has the nest
In the arbor vitae now?"

I breathe the sweet spring
Smell of hyacinths
And white and purple lilacs.
The stone steps are warm.
I lean into a corner,
Sun seeping into my body
Like heated syrup
Soaking into pancakes.

A space of time my own –
For just this moment
I belong to sun and earth
And birds and sky.
Eyes closed, I feel
And hear and smell
God's world around me –
And know that it's enough.

Evolution

My daughter is coming
To spend some time with us
This coming spring.
I see her seldom, now
That we live so far apart,
And, because we are friends
At last, I miss her.

I think of all those years
When she was growing up
And, yes, older and married.
We had so many problems,
She and I, so many issues
We couldn't seem to solve,
No matter what!

We fought and cried – said
Such hurtful things! She seemed
Only hateful, trying her wings,
Scornful of us, her teachers,
And all who truly thought
We wished her well. Even then,
There were times she needed us.

A late night call in tears –
"Mom, could you come get me?"
And, of course, I would.
I sat and held her hand.
At home, in cars, in hospitals.
But soon enough, we were
Angry with each other again!

Years passed, as they are wont to do,
And time has changed us both.
Like children, taking baby steps,
We've both tried out new ways
To trust each other once again,
And find a mother-daughter bond,
The precious caring that we'd lost.

We've stumbled oft, slipped into
Worn out ways too many times.
But now we climb back up
And try again. Little by little we've
Formed a new definition of "us."
Finally, together, we have built
A bridge, a strong and lasting love.

SUMMER

Our Garden –
My Dad's and Mine

The weeds pull easily from
The damp earth, and the rich, loamy
Aroma fills my nostrils as I
Finger-comb the matted leaves
From last year's dead tangle, uncovering
Bright green new growth hiding there.

My father was the gardener. I see him
Bending over his roses, carefully pruning,
Holding a rose, and breathing deeply.
I watch as he teaches me which are weeds
To pull and which are the tender
Shoots of flowers, reaching for the light.

During the cold and snowy months of winter
I'd often find him buried in garden
Catalogues and poring over his charts,
Laying out with ruler, in measured sections, his
Summer garden – which colors,
Which heights, what foliage for best effect?

And then, come summer, the rewards!
A constant flow of color into color,
And my dad, happily cutting flowers for the
Living room, the dining table, the sun porch,

Always flowers that bloomed with the rich
Perfume of such a labor of love!

Although he is no longer here, I feel
His spirit beside me when I garden.
Although I do not lay out my plot with
Such precision, still I find his eye
Within my own, searching out that flow
Of colors and patterns to please us both!

I weed, I turn my compost, I trim and prune,
I water and fertilize, as I watched him do –
Cheering the early blooms of bulbs,
Enjoying the showy flowers of spring and, later,
Summer's profusion, storing memories to stay
Until it's time for catalogues again!

Peace

Like my Himalayan cat,
The fog curls around me,
Licking at my face.
Whiteness and quiet peace
Surround me.
I hear the waves
Lapping gently at the shore,
But I cannot see them.

I walk tentatively,
My feet unsure of steps
Taken in an empty space –
Empty of people,
Empty of distance,
Empty of sounds
Except the muted whisper
Of the waves.

The calm seeps into me.
My mind is still,
Conflicting thoughts erased,
Until, the peace complete,
The dampness turns me back,
And I see my shadow house
Appearing in the fog.
My morning coffee waits.

Martha's Vineyard Vacation

Up with the children at seven
For blueberry pancakes and ham.
Flapjacks enough for eleven –
How many will fit in the pan?

Lay out some slices of bread.
Spread with egg salad maybe,
Some tuna and celery for Fred,
And a "p,b and j" for the baby!

Fetch from the line all the towels
And swimsuits hanging to dry.
Ignore the grumbles and scowls
About sunscreen you have to apply.

Stack the pop in the ice chest.
With sandwiches, yogurt and fruit.
Pack napkins, chips and the rest
In the picnic basket to suit.

Pile out, and head for the seashore
With picnic, umbrella and chairs!
No room for anything more –
But then, nobody really cares!

Oh, joy! What a day at the beach!
We swim, jump the waves, and tan,
Drink our soda, eat a peach,
Its edges trimmed with sand!

Alack! Alas! It's time to go!
Our homeward way we wend,
Not sad at all because we know
Tomorrow we'll do it again!

Upside-Down Town

Not a ripple disturbs the
Surface of Sunset Lake.
In the bright sun
I squint across the pond,
And there I see my town
In the water mirror,
Upside down!
Houses standing on their roofs,
Their colors bleeding greens
And grays and yellows like
Paints on a silver-blue
Impressionistic canvas.

The gnarled branches
Of the oaks and maples,
Instead of reaching skyward,
Stretch their leafy fingers
Toward the bottom of the lake,
As if fishing for their lunch!

Upside down cars whiz by
Above the houses,

Wheels spinning in the air.
A patch of feathery yellow reeds
Grows down, not up, and
Sweeps the sandy depths.

Do you suppose that people
In those topsy-turvy houses
Are standing on their heads?
Or walking on the ceilings
Just as Mary Poppins did?

Maybe they just float,
Like astronauts in space,
And drink their soda
Through a straw and eat
From drifting plates!
It's disorienting, yes,
To say the very least!

I really think I like
My town much better
Right side up!

July

The sun's so hot it shimmers
Through humid, pulsing air,
And beach sand burns the feet
Of children hopping there.
There's a more than fragrant odor
Of coconut oil and lotion.
Umbrellas sprout like flowers
On the shore beside the ocean!

As for myself, I like to swim
When the afternoon's cooled down,
And crowds have all gone home
Or else have left for town.
If it's hot I'd rather read
On the shady, breezy porch
And leave the other people
To sun themselves and scorch!

I love the smell of barbecue
That wafts along the breeze.
I think I'll call my neighbor
And ask to try some, please!
Yes, July's a time for leisure
To do whate'er you will
So, decide to DO or NOT to do –
Whatever fills the bill!

Fog

The fog lies deep,
Deep as a whisper,
On Sengekontacket pond,
The far shore only a
Charcoal smudge
Engulfed in smoky gray.

At left, the scrubby dunes
Hunch dark along the road.
The sea beyond blends
Seamlessly into the void,
Where tolls the warning
Of a passing, phantom ship.

Then, ahead, out of the mist,
A pair of yellow eyes!
And a dark and formless beast
Slips by me on the road, silently,
Disappearing, winking red
In my rear view mirror.

When I reach the little bridge,
Suddenly the air is clear!
No trace of fog or misty trees
Or passing, ghostly ships!
Without a thought, I turn
And head back whence I came!

I stop along the sandy road,
Take up my steaming cup,
And scramble through the dunes.
I sit, heedless of the damp sand,
Sip my morning coffee,
And listen – listen to the silence.

How Many

How many years is it
From the long past decades
When we were young
And brought our children
To Martha's Vineyard?

I often think "How many?"
How many pails of clams dug,
How many dozens of crabs netted,
How many pounds of mussels
Picked from the rocks?

How many kinds of fish
Wrestled in, gutted and filleted?
How many baskets of blueberries,
Or bags of wild grapes picked,
Or rose hips or strawberries?

How many dinners eaten of
Clams, crabs, and mussels
Dripping in melted butter?
How many dozens of jars
Of jams and jellies, carefully tended?

Where are the children now?
Grown and moved away.
Few crabs now live in the pond,
Some clam beds closed for pollution,
Some mussels still, but smaller.

Many places we loved to pick
The wild blueberries and grapes
Built up now with homes,

Even the once wide beaches
Eroding with each storm!

So much has passed, but oh!
How many things remain!
Like our beloved ocean isle,
We ourselves have changed
And now have different dreams.

And so I think – how many yet
Of pink and gold Menemsha sunsets
And sunny beach days?
How many roses and beach plums to see,
And shifting ocean views?

How many drinks on the porch
And jokes and chats with friends?
How many velvet foggy morns,
Birds crowding at the feeders
And squabbling in the trees?

How many blazing autumns
And blue October skies?
How many blankets of snow and
Warm lilac rains? It really doesn't matter
For we'll treasure every one!

My Name is Rain

My name is rain
But I have many faces.

I am the howling gale
That rattles your shutters
And sends the porch chairs
Skittering across the floor.
I whistle and scream
And drive cascades of water
Against your windows
And down the rain gutters,
Forcing tiny rivulets
Between the shingles
To drip tinnily into buckets
On the floor.

I am shy and quiet,
Misty and mysterious.
I cushion and muffle
The busy noise of life.
My voice is a whisper
Scarcely heard.
My tiny droplets
Fall like downy feathers,
Tickling the upturned faces
Of flowers and children
And lovers
Walking hand in hand.

I am the steady, drenching rain
That soaks the parched ground
And awakes the sleeping

Iris and daffodil
Crocus and tulip.
I tend the farmer's crops
And green the fields
And pastures.
I softly beat my drum
In rhythm on your roof
And lull you to sleep
And pleasant dreams.

I am the summer storm
Sweeping in suddenly
Without warning
From the West.
I bring the fireworks
Of crackling thunder
And lightning blazes
That limn the trees
In stark relief,
That send cats and children
Scurrying under beds
With eyes clenched shut.

I am as old as the earth
And as young as spring
I can be harsh and loud
Or so gentle that
Children cavort and splash
In my muddy puddles.
Farmers rejoice.
I send picnickers,
Laughing and wet,
To have their picnic
Under a river's bridge.
I am both feared and loved.

My name is rain,
And I have many faces.

AUTUMN

Communication Lines

Stretching from pole to pole
Along the country road,
The black wires sway
And sing in the wind,
Carrying a thousand voices
Unheard by those
Who walk, heedless,
Unmindful, far below.

A desperate young woman
Calls her mother.
"The baby has a fever.
What shall I do?"
A love-struck young girl
Cries joyously to her friend,
"I think he loves me!"
Across the world
A businessman
Calls in an order
For 100 computers,
Delivery expedited!

And high above are
Communications of another sort!
The long thin lines
Are crowded with
Pushy, chattering birds.
What adventures do they tell?
Do they give directions to
That far-off summer place,
Now that fall is here?
Or do they merely gossip.
As we mortals often do,
About their neighbors?

The slender lines sway
In the wind, alive with birds
Alive with voices! Listen!
If you stand very still,
Beneath the chatter
Of the avian flock above,
You can hear the hum
Of a thousand conversations!

Nor'Easter

The waves dash themselves
Against the rocks,
Sending geysers of spray
High over the seawall,
Half drowning the cars
That are creeping slowly
Through the sandy lakes
Forming on the road.
The wind screams
And pounds its fists in a
Tantrum on car windows.
The angry sea hisses
And spits a frothy foam
Onto the curling mountains of
Emerald and blue-black water.
A lone cormorant dips and bobs,
Appears and disappears
In the unaccustomed,
Roiling surface of the salt
Pond across the road.
Beyond, the trees whip and
Thrash their arms,
Moaning and keening
In the driving sheets of rain.
Pieces of their shattered limbs
Litter the roadway, and
A single strand of wire
Flips back and forth,
Sparking red in the gloom.
People park their cars
Away from falling limbs
And dash for leaf-strewn
Porches, chairs all spun awry.
They shed their dripping coats
And watch the raging storm
Wreak havoc, safely, from inside!

October Days

Fluttering, turning, floating
Across the autumn sky,
Gold and scarlet and apple-sweet
The leaf-like days drift by.
Lazy days of bittersweet
When time stands almost still,
But harvest moon and crisp night air
Bring a hint of the coming chill.

Rake them in! Gather them up
As a miser hoards his gold,
As a squirrel hides his acorns
Against the bitter cold.
For the lazy, golden, cinnamon days
When time stood almost still
Will warm your heart 'til a misty night
Brings an end to winter's will.

My Apple Tree

They're cutting down my apple tree.
Well, I say it was mine, even
Though it was in a neighbor's field.
She never minded that we climbed
In it, and we often did,
Being such tomboys as we were!
The branches were just low enough
For a ten year old to jump up
And grasp, to shinny up the trunk.
We didn't have a swing set or
A fancy playground nearby –
We lived in the country after all!
So we played in the hayloft and
Wandered the woods and fields
And clambered around in our
Apple tree jungle gym!
We swung hand over hand from
One branch to another.
We hung by our knees
From the lowest limb and
Then, bravely, from just our heels,
Where we could drop to the ground
On our hands and knees
And think we had accomplished
A dangerous acrobatic feat!
One day a limb broke, and
I fell flat on my stomach,
Knocking the wind out of me!
I was sure I'd never breathe again,

But I lived to climb another day,
Not even daunted by the scare!
And then there were the apples!
Mostly windfalls, with some bruises
And the occasional worm!
We gathered them in baskets
And helped cut up the apples,
Cook them soft – reveling in
The smell and taste of summer –
And can glass jars of applesauce
For winter. If we were lucky,
(And we usually were!)
There would be some of the warm,
Pink, cinnamony sauce left that
We could scrape right out of the kettle.

Now the tree is gnarled and brittle.
Some of the branches bare of leaves,
The apples small and wormy,
So they're cutting my old friend down.
I take home a bag full of apple chips
To toss in the fire on a winter evening,
To close my eyes and smell the sweet
Applewood smoke rising, and reminisce!

Tantrum!

The wind is having a tantrum.
It whines and screams and
Howls around the house,
Tearing at the shingles,
Whacking the roof with branches,
Blowing porch chairs into a corner,
A loose cushion into a puddle
On the next block over!
It throws the recycle bin
Into the raspberry bushes
So cans and bottles litter the yard.
It sends trash can covers
Skittering across the road
To land against the fence!
It snaps tree limbs like pick-up sticks
And angrily summons the rain
To slash against the windows
With little icy pellets and
Drive water in under the sill
To form a puddle on the floor!
Probably tomorrow it will clear,
And we'll all go outside
To clean up the debris!
But the mischievous, childish wind
Will have the last laugh –
Because who can punish the wind
For the mess it made!

Dawn at Farm Pond

The thin skin of ice
That coats the brown stubble
Crackles and splinters
Like shards of glass
Beneath my feet.
On trees and shrubs
Necklaces of crystal beads
Reflect the day's new sun
In rainbow prisms
That dance beyond, to where
A peach and rosy sky
Has been upended in
The honey-golden mirror
Of the pond,
And clouds, like
Great white swans,
Swim slowly from my sight.
I feel my breath come sharp.
These earth-bound eyes
With which I see
Fill up with tears,
That I'm allowed
Such beauty, given free!

Wind-Puppy

Like a cantankerous puppy,
Dancing in circles around me,
The wind whines and whimpers,
Demanding my attention!
It teases as I walk, pulling
At my flapping coat-tails!

Leaping for my scarf,
It nearly knocks me down!
It noses up my pantlegs
And then my sleeves.
It nips my fingers and toes
With its sharp teeth.

I turn into my driveway,
And, just that suddenly,
The puppy-wind grows tired.
It circles me wearily
A few more times, lies down
At my feet, and goes to sleep!

A Cardboard Box Tumbles...

A cardboard box tumbles
Down the dark and empty street.
Cold gray houses stand watch,
No life within, their voices stilled,
Their wide eyes vacant.
On the porches furniture shrouds
Flap and tear in the bitter wind.
Dry leaves swirl and whisper.

Do these sentinels remember?
Do they see a different time?
Are they not waiting
For the children's laughter,
The banging screen door,
The clatter of skateboards,
People calling from the street?

Do they long for summer?
Sweet, salty air blowing
Through their open doors?
The smell of beach roses?
The squeaking of a porch swing?
Do they recall a warmth of sun
Soaking into their brittle,
Cold, arthritic bones?

For now, though, they stand waiting,
Staring down the empty street,
Watching the cardboard box
Tumbling end over end
Along the dusty road,
Watching the dry leaves swirl
And spin into small tornadoes,
Watching for summer.

43

Promise

The November air is chill.
Shredded, racing clouds
Look down upon
Half-naked trees below.
Brown, yellow, red,
The leaves are torn
From Mother Tree's grasp
And fall panicked,
Dizzy, to huddle on
The cold, gray walk.

Finally, raked into piles,
Their fate is sealed,
The bonfire lit.
Red-gold sparkles
Fly swirling upward
In a smoky cloud,
To flicker out
In the night sky,
Leaving behind them
Only ashes of memories

But Mother Tree,
Bending in the wind, silent,
Keeps her secret,
Waiting out the long
Gestation time of winter,
Pregnant already with
The green and tender
Babes of spring.
Awaiting patiently
The promise of rebirth.

HUMOR & WHIMSEY

Blank

I have a blank white sheet
On which to write my thoughts.
But it glares right back at me,
And ideas I have naught!

I sit at my computer
And look around the room.
My brain is just as empty
As if I'd swept it with a broom!

At last I just start typing
Whatever comes to mind.
Be it letters or just nonsense,
Perhaps a thought I'll find!

The jottings make no sense;
I'm completely at a loss!
This is just a waste of time,
And this effort I should toss!

However, just as suddenly
I find ideas flowing
From fingertips to keyboard –
I don't know where it's going!

A feeling of direction comes.
Inspiration's leading me
To a place I'd not expected!
At last my words run free!

Art Show

All around the walls
The multi colors sail,
Unfurled for all to see
And judge and buy –
Or maybe not!
They catch the eye
Of passers-by
Who come to stare
And have some wine.
Perhaps a bite,
And socialize a bit –
Or maybe not!
Some stop and take the time
To look and really see,
To travel 'round
The sea of sails
And find their muse –
Or maybe not!
We'll meet new friends,
Some browsers,
Perhaps some artists, too.
We'll have some fun
And sell a lot –
Or maybe not!

Mystery Lady

Who is it I see
In the mirror today?
Who is that lady
With hair of gray?

Who is that woman
With wrinkly skin
And brownish spots
And a double chin?

It's surely not I –
It must be a joke!
Perhaps I've dreamt
And haven't awoke!

For I look young
And smooth of skin.
I'm clear of eye
And certainly thin!

So who's that lady
Whose image I see?
Of one thing I'm certain –
It isn't me!

Hair

Hairdos come and hairdos go,
As snapshots in our albums show.
Once were pompadours and wigs,
Some were powdered, some just BIG!

The beehive had its fling at life
Before succumbing to the knife.
Pageboys, shags, and Afros frizzy
Kept the stylists in a tizzy.

Women tried to look their best
When even fads were at their crest.
We've had sassoons and pixie cuts
And curly tops, but straight is what

The girls now want, with tresses that
Hang like curtains. Get a hat!!!
The strands hang wispy in the eyes
Or ponytails, half caught with ties.

The new −mown locks, called "layered" now,
Hang lank and stringy by the brow,
"Finger-combed" with crooked parts
Like cowpaths made by oxen carts.

No more styles to suit the face,
Just hanging hair that has no grace.
When can we see some beauty back?
Is pride of self the thing we lack?

Committee Buzz

The air is thick with words.
They flutter and beat
About my ears
Like a thousand moths!
A proliferation of pontification
And pedantic pomposities
Numbs my mind
And muddles my thoughts.
Details, details, details!
Minute subtleties and
Nuances confuse, confound!
I feel the urge to shout,
"Simple! Keep it simple!
Give up the cluttered verbiage!
Give us advantages!
Disadvantages!
Points we need
To make a decision!"
The words retreat into
A hum of beating wings.
I smile vacantly
And think of something else!

My Dentist

Some people really hate to make
A trip to the dentist's chair.
They dread the thought and quake
To think what happens there

They fear the needle and the drills,
That awful jabbing in the jaw –
That scary whining as he fills
And stretches WIDE your maw!

But if my dentist you should see
You wouldn't feel the bane.
His witty conversation helps,
And I don't feel any pain.

He's oh, so gentle, full of care,
Deflecting all my fears.
He carefully explains each step
So there won't be any tears.

While Dr. Herman's dentist chair
Is not my favorite place,
If I have to go, then I'll arrive
With a smile upon my face!

Politics

Politics, politics!
Speculation runs rampant!
Words, and more words!
Slurs, lies, truths
And half-truths!
What is the truth?
Does anyone know?
If anyone knows,
Who is it?
Commentators, pundits
Speak loudly
And argue endlessly.
Reporters on the scene
Give us the "inside dope!"
Oh, really?
Is what they show us
Unslanted, unbiased,
Or does it merely
Justify a point of view?
Pork and more pork!
What's mine is mine and
What's yours is mine!
Graft, inside deals, corruption –
Where do *we* fit in?
Those of us who work,
Or used to, until we
Lost our jobs, our homes,
Our self-esteem?
We try to make our views,
Our pain, known –
We write letters, make calls!
Is anybody listening
Or is it all just
Politics as usual?

A Brief Ballad About Wine

I think I might be called,
In the contemporary lexicon,
Alcohol-challenged!
One glass of wine finds me
Crawling on the floor giggling
While I look for the glasses
I left on the table, or, worse,
Snoozing loudly on the couch,
Or, worst of all, holding
My head with both hands,
Hoping the pain will not kill me!
On a hot day recently, I ran into,
On the ferry, someone I knew,
Who generously brought me
A large glass of white wine!
(I might add that it had been a
Long day with little breakfast
And a very light lunch!)
I thanked him, sipped and chatted
And made a point of emptying the glass
Because, after all, I wanted to be polite!
Hmm! Not bad at all! No headache,
I wasn't talking nonsense or giggling,
And I didn't fall asleep! But alas!
The ferry docked, and I stood up!
Oops! The boat, although not moving,
Seemed to be rolling side to side!
Righting myself with a little effort,
I walked with exaggerated care
Down the long aisle to the off-ramp
And up the dock to the waiting car,
All the while feeling as if I were

Putting my feet down on
Large, soft sponges that
Kept moving just out of reach!
Realizing that I was quite looped,
I could only hope my sparkling attempts
To participate in conversation
Were making some sort of sense!
Upon arriving home, I graciously
Thanked my benefactor once more,
Let myself into the house, sat down
In the living room chair,
And fell asleep for two hours!

AT HOME

From the Other Room

I hear him in the kitchen.
A knife clinks on a plate.
I smell an odor rich in
Garlic, herbs and steak.
And then a happy song I hear –
A pseudo-operatic voice
Is singing loud and clear.
(I wonder at his choice!)
He mimics Jolson or Goulet –
I wince a bit when, oft,
I hear the words are true,
But the key is slightly off!
Sometimes I grow impatient
But I know a certain thing –
I'd miss my entertainment
If my husband didn't sing!

Puzzle

The giant jigsaw puzzle
On the table in the den
Entices me to hustle
Back to work on it again.

I've put the box's cover
On the floor beside the chair
So I can't look it over
And see the picture there.

I sort out all the edges,
Then pieces of some grass,
A part that looks like hedges –
Some sky, some window glass.

I love to see the landscape
Unfold before my eyes –
A garden, then a cottage
I think I recognize.

Is that a little girl
There walking on a path?
That gold might be a curl,
The red could be a sash.

Above, some branches reach
To touch a sun that sinks
In streaks of fiery peach
And yellows, reds, and pinks.

I wonder why the action
Of fitting in each piece
Gives me such satisfaction and
From problems gives surcease!

My Refuge

The kitchen is my refuge
When a respite's what I need!
From the never-ending deluge
Of daily wants I'm freed.

I mix the oil and sweetening,
The nutmeg, flour and salt.
Add oats or chips or nuts in
With milk, and beat it all!

The warm and spicy smell
Is wonderful to savor,
But then we have, as well,
That so-delicious flavor.

Perhaps I'll mix some bread up
And set it out to rise
Until it fills the bowl up –
That yeast smell gets the prize!

I love to cook for company
A special dinner treat.
Perhaps a gourmet recipe –
Souffle or trifle sweet.

I really need to clean out
The cellar and the shed,
But I think I'll turn about
And bake a cake instead!

There's dust on every table.
The mending's piling high.
I'll do it when I'm able,
But right now I'll bake a pie!

Home Movies

Family movies –
Bore, bore, bore!
Haven't I seen
This program before?

Voices babbling,
Musical tunes,
No one listening,
Birthday balloons!

Presents unwrapping,
There's Uncle Joe.
No, it's his brother!
And there's little Flo!

The baby's so cute –
She's got a new tooth.
There's this one and that one –
Enough now, forsooth!!

We lived it, enjoyed it,
And had a great time.
But hours of it over
And over's a crime!

Home Movies II

They always want to see them
Whenever they come home –
The movies of the "olden days"
Before they left to roam.

"Show the ones of Christmas
Or the baby ones of me
Or times on Martha's Vineyard
On the beaches by the sea."

We marvel at how young we were.
We gambolled in the waves,
Made faces at the camera,
And built sea-creature caves.

We laugh at all the birthdays,
Baby hands all frosted cake –
We point out all the relatives –
Who's that, for goodness' sake!

The Christmases of long ago
Show up with gifts galore!
We're still in our pajamas,
Piles of wrappings on the floor!

It doesn't seem that long ago –
Those days so far behind –
And the movies bring them back,
As we watch the past unwind.

Insomniac

I lie in bed, almost asleep,
But my mind has other ideas
And begins to mull over
Everything in my life!
Suddenly, I am wide awake.
I turn on my side and fluff my pillow
To get more comfortable.
I resolve not to think about anything,
Make my mind a blank!
But my feet are cold! I sit up
And pick up socks from the floor
And pull them on. That's better!
I stretch out flat on my back
And try relaxing all my muscles
From the top of my head down,
As I've been taught. Doesn't work!
I turn on my side and curl up.
I breathe deeply – once, twice –
Oh! Oh! Oh! A cramp
In my calf pulls me upright, and
I leap out of bed onto the icy floor.
Flexing my foot and leg, I limp
Painfully back and forth
Around the room.
 I approach the bed again,
With trepidation, and smooth the
Blankets and pillow just right,
Wooing sleep. But no! Still,
Questions float through my head –
"Did I...?" "How will ...?"

"If I organize it this way, then..."
"Stop! Stop! Stop!"
I tell myself. I try humming
To drown out my thoughts!
Now I'm too warm. I toss off
A blanket and throw the socks
Back on the floor,
Untangle my blankets
And punch my pillow! It's no use.
I get up, tie on my robe,
And go downstairs to the kitchen
To make a cup of chamomile.
While I'm waiting for the tea
I eat two crackers, two cookies
And some ice cream
I spoon right from the container.
I carry my cup carefully into
The dark living room, settle
Myself on the couch by the window,
And watch the patterns
Made by the wind and trees
In the park across the street.
The steaming tea, the monotony and
Dark hypnotize me,
And finally I relax.
I trudge wearily up the stairs,
Crawl back into bed,
Pull up my blankets,
And fall well and soundly asleep!

Nemesis

I close my eyes to sleep,
When suddenly I hear
A buzzing in my bedroom –
It's right here by my ear!

It's over by the window –
No, it's by me on the floor.
Now it's quiet. Is it stopping
So I can rest? Oh, no!

That buzzing starts again.
I click the light on high,
And there's my nemesis!
A black and greenish fly!

It's climbing up the curtain.
My magazine is near.
I fold it in my hand –
Buzz, buzz again I hear!

Where did that nuisance go?
It's landing on the lamp!
Ka-thwack! I hit the shade,
But the pesky thing's decamped!

And now it's buzzing merrily
Upon the window pane.
Another chance I get. Ka-whack!
I try for it again!

I pull away the weapon,
But there's no fly beneath.
It's over on the bureau!
My frustration has increased!

I see it on the doorjamb,
And quickly do my best.
I lunge and smack!! I've got it!
At last I'll get some rest!

Old-time Movie

He's seen this movie many times,
Each time as rapt as last!
He tells me, "Watch, watch here!
What happens next comes fast!"

I try to read to shut it out,
But he doesn't have a heart.
It's, "Look at this exciting scene!
Wait! Here's a special part!"

I guess the subtle nuances
Escape my wandering mind,
For much as I enjoyed this film –
Oh, please, do not rewind!

I must admit I've had enough
Of recalling and dissecting.
How can I bear to watch again
These "classics" he's collecting!

MUSINGS

Solitude

I am cloaked in silence that
Flows out from my solitude
In all directions and fills
The space around me.
Its healing presence seeps
Into my heart and mind,
My deepest inner core.

No sound of any kind,
Not even the subtle humming
Of the refrigerator,
Interrupts my thoughts.
No traffic noise, no telephone,
No background music disturbs
The calm that soothes my soul.

I need this quiet time each day
To reacquaint me with myself!
The stresses of my life,
For now, are held at bay.
In these few moments of renewal,
This time of replenishment,
I find the strength I need.

Empty

A hammock swings to and fro in the wind
As if propelled by an unseen foot.
A tricycle lies abandoned by the porch,
One handle grip with its multicolored
Streamers long gone, a wheel missing,
Its once-resplendent pink paint eaten with rust.

The "For Sale" sign is old. It sways tipsily,
Tilting in the wind, covered in graffiti.
Where is the little girl who used to play
In this lonely and forsaken yard?
Where is the boy who whiled away the hours
Reading and dreaming in the hammock?

Where is the mother who tended these gardens,
Now full of weeds, and the father whose children
Greeted him joyfully at the end of the day?
What calamitous series of disasters
Befell this family, to force them out,
To make them leave the home they loved?

Maybe they sleep now in cheap motels and
Eat their frugal meal at a breakfast bar
Or live in a noisy, overcrowded shelter.
Or do they move from place to place,
Rootless, living in a car, dreaming of that
Joy-filled home they left behind, a lifetime ago?

The staring house now stands bereft,
Bewildered, wondering – where is the family that
Once lived and loved inside its empty shell?
It seems to wait in loneliness, pining for
Those happier days of oh, so long ago,
While the hammock swings to and fro in the wind.

Lost Muse

If I could somehow creep
Inside my brain and mind
And wander through the neurons
I wonder what I'd find.

Is a jumble there of words
All begging to be found
And strings of clever phrases
Just waiting to confound?

And, slith'ring through the spaces,
In shades of every hue.
Are there slippery ideas that are
Trying to get through?

Are there empty pathways there
Where words and thoughts collide
And then, like magic, morph
Into a flowing tide

Of tumbling, wordy rivers
That spill and swirl and splash
Over all the rocks and blocks?
Would it happen in a flash?

Or would it take me days
Of thinking, sweat and toil,
And scrambling o'er the boulders
Along the river's coil

To find among the brainwaves
A way that I could choose –
A path at last that beckoned me
To find my errant muse!

Silence

You sit across from me.
I speak.
Your abstract smile
And nod of head
Convey to me
You haven't
Really heard
A word I said.

"That's nice'" you say,
And, turning back
To your news, remark,
"The market went down
Again today."
I cannot bear for you
To close me out.
Please turn around.

See me! I need you
To touch me. I reach
But cannot span the gulf
That stretches wide
Between us! Help me!
But you do not hear.
You do not even know
I died.

Too Hard to Write

I cannot write.
Not too few thoughts,
But too many,
Whirling, twisting
In my mind –
Too many fears,
Too many doubts!
The channels of
My mind are choked,
Like leaf-clogged gutters,
With formless words
That pour over and
Are wasted on the
Barren ground beneath.
Fears fly around
My head and knit
My words into knots
That ravel into strings
Of nothingness.
When will this nightmare
Cease, the fears subside?
Where can I hide?
I feel the worst is yet to come,
And yet I need to fight
This feeling of despair!
And so I try to tell myself
That time will pass –
That this brief moment in
Eternity will someday
Be only a memory.
But will I ever truly
Be at peace? I cannot tell.

Anguish

Anguish! Agonizing!
More than ache or hurt,
More than sharp,
Knife-twisting pain!
Not a physical,
Grit your teeth and bear it
Kind of pain, but
A searing laceration
Of the mind that
Rends the very soul
And leaves it groping
In the bottomless pit
Of dark despair.
I wail, begging
Surcease from terror,
From panic that
Devours the heart and soul
And leaves me pleading,
Yet dry of tears.
The universe seems empty –
No solace! No respite
In this, the heart's
Darkest moment,
Nightmare of
Collected fears,
Pressing down, smothering!
Ripping apart life
And foolish dreams!
I pray for end of night.

Odyssey

It's a five-hour round trip,
What with the ferry, shuttle, a
Twenty-minute walk, sometimes the bus,
Just to see him for a couple of hours.
Sometimes he's not doing well
Or is sleeping while I'm there.
It's been such a long time!
First there was the back operation.
They said it went well, that soon I
Could see him in the recovery room.
But then he had the stroke!

Those weeks in intensive care
When they kept asking him
Every hour if he knew his name,
His birthday, his middle name,
The president, the year!
At least he could answer, if
Only haltingly. When the pain
Was dulled, he slept,
So lethargic it was scary!
He developed pneumonia,
Fluid around the lungs, too,
And had to have a drain,
Along with all the IVs,
And so many tests! EEGs,
X-rays, scans, ultrasounds,
Over and over again!

Finally, release to a room
Out of the ICU, but still tubes

And tests and more tests!
We sat by his bed, day after day,
Watching him sleep or trying
To engage him in conversation.
Putting his bed up, putting it down,
Getting nurses to reposition him,
Wetting his mouth with sponges,
Taking turns to get a break.
Then, after thirty-one days,

At last, to the rehab hospital!
Progress, pain, setbacks, complaints
(Who wouldn't complain?)
At present he's making small steps.
He is able to swallow all right,
So no more pureed food!
He can stand for a short time
In the standing frame,
A little longer this week than last!
The physical therapy is slow and
Sometimes discouraging,
Retraining those unused muscles.

Certainly it will be many weeks yet,
But now I can see a future when
He will come back home to us,
To me and to his beloved
Bernese Mountain Dog, Andy,
And his cats, Sweetie Pie and Sophie,
And he'll be back to his old self again!

Lilies

The lilies were a surprise!
One white flower, petals curling,
Greenish buds just starting to open,
Sweet aroma filling the house!
A gift from a friend who
Knew I was downhearted –
Who understood the angst that
Pursued, that wriggled in
Underneath my breastbone,
That made me want to hide!

My friend is one who never
Told me to "buck up",
That many others had a harder row,
That I should be grateful
For the things I have!
Who never said, "Don't worry!"
Who never tried to cheer me
With false hopes, who never
Judged or compared my woes
To her much greater sacrifice!

This friend brought me lilies
To fill my house and weary soul
With loveliness, to lift
My battered spirits with
A sheer and simple beauty
I'd not seen, for blindness
Of self-pity, worry, fear,
In my paralysis of dark!
My friend brought me lilies
And a lightness for my heart!

One Day at a Time!

Why can I not write?
I am overwhelmed
By the minutiae of everyday life!
Dawn comes, and I awake,
But no!
I pull the covers over m head
And close my eyes tightly
Against the coming day.
I am not ready yet!

When I can avoid it no longer
I sit up and dress, reluctantly,
Take the dog out, bring
Him in and feed him,
Give him fresh water.
Give him his pills and
Spray his poor shaven rat tail
With anti-itch lotion,
(He has a hot spot!)
And put some ointment on it.

I fix some breakfast, wash it
Down with yesterday's coffee.
Take the cats some fresh water,
Get them their breakfast,

And clean the litter,
Wipe Sweetie Pie's eyes
And put drops in them.
I'll comb out both Sophie
And Sweetie Pie later on.
I make my bed and
Clean up the dishes,
Get out my big green backpack
And put Doug's clean clothes in it.

Oops! I forgot to start the laundry
I brought home yesterday!
It's already 10:30, and I
Have to leave by five to eleven!
Spray on the sun lotion,
Check that I have my Patriot ferry
Pass and the SPF 50 lip balm
Doug asked me to get.
It's hot and humid, but I trudge
Twenty minutes to the ferry
For the half-hour boat ride
That I actually enjoy!
Just me, the water, sun and breeze
For 30 minutes of peace
For my not-so-quiet mind.

Three hours for lunch with Doug,
Bring him up-to-date with
All the news of friends and family,
Watch him in physical therapy
And learn what I will have
To do in a few weeks
When he gets home!

Back to the van,
Back to the Patriot ferry,
And another brief time for myself.
I walk home, hot and tired.
Take Andy out, finish the laundry
And hang it out on the line.
I think it won't rain tonight.

Run to the store for some
Necessities, cat food in
particular
Check the e-mail, answer notes,
Water the parched garden
Take Andy for a walk, and
Then feed him his dinner.
Time for MY dinner, but what?

Let's see. I sauté a couple of
Chicken tenders in the small pan,
Slice up a whole tomato,
Add cantaloupe, cottage cheese,
Eat some of it and fall asleep
In the chair in front of the
Fan on its highest setting.
I wake up with a start and make
Myself get up, clean the kitchen.

Afterwards, I watch a couple
Of mindless television shows
While I make mental lists
Of what I have to do the next day.

Finally, I feed the cats again,
Take Andy out once more,
Wash myself up and fall into bed,
Where I lie awake for hours,
Going over everything
That's happening in my life.
At last I fall into a fitful sleep.
I'll deal with tomorrow
When it comes!

Darkness

Inside my box
The night is very dark.
A chill wind blows through my mind
And scatters thoughts
Like dry leaves before a storm –
Twisting, whirling out of reach.
They pile up in corners in
Disordered heaps.
I grasp in panic, but they
Skitter away just out of reach,
Taunting me. Please!
Bring back my ordered life!
I'm lost in moonless black –
No light ahead – no warmth –
All order gone! I shiver.
I draw in upon myself
And see me growing smaller
And smaller – until, at last,
I simply disappear.

Forgiving

Resentment and anger
Scratch and gnaw
Like mice around the edges
Of my mouse-trap mind
That won't spring shut,
But lies in wait
While I compose
Self-righteous messages
I exhale in fiery ash,
Only to vanish in the air
Like failed smoke signals,
Never to reach a destination!
Instead, whirling in and
Around my pounding head,
They push farther away
The solace of the sleep I seek!
Where is reason?
Where is forgiveness?
Is giving's purpose to receive?
Is getting something back
A reward for dutiful diligence?
Or is the joy of giving
A special present of its own?
Snap shut, mouse-trap mind!
Throw your ugly contents out!
Douse the embers of resentment
With rivers of forgiveness,
To heal my soul and heart.

Acceptance

Poems – rhyming or
Free verse – straightforward,
Which paint a picture
That makes us laugh or cry,
That strikes a chord within us!
Not ordinary! Not untaught
Or unlearned! None of those!
I used to think that others
Were on a higher plane,
That only abstractions,
(Words, ideas, strung together
In concepts a mystery to me,
Forming no connections
In my more linear mind),
Were "real," "insightful!"
(Deep, obscure, and meaningful
Being one and the same)
While I, somehow more literal,
Must somehow be inferior
In intelligence or understanding!
But I've grown old enough to find
That all of us seek meaning differently,
That I, writing in clearer, plainer,
Less convoluted language,
Still can scale the heights and
Depths of understanding,
Still communicate in simple words
Which stir the heart and mind
And reflect a deeper meaning
For those who wish to see.

REMINISCENCES

Time

Like a shimmery satin
Ribbon blowing in the wind
Time slips and twists,
Its meaning constantly shifting.
How much time is there?
Do we have time? How long?
Can space be time? Is there
Only a certain space of time
In which we are caught, live
Out our lifespan and die?

There is a certain time,
To catch a train, a set time
For an appointment.
How long is a stretch of time?
Is time enough just enough
Or more than enough?
Is it an hour, a week, a year?
Is an eon still time?
Does time have weight?
Can it weigh heavily on someone?

When is there not enough time?
A day to take a trip?
A month to pay bills?
Is time longer or shorter
When you don't have the money?
How can time be short for
One person and long for another?
Is a long time heavy or light?

What about a moment in history?
Is the moment time?
Is history time or is it space?

So, what IS time? Is it flexible?
A perception? An idea? How can
Time be both exact and inexact!
Clock pendulums swing, but
They tick off only the hours,
And minutes and seconds,
Never the elastic, elusive time
Which spins its own thread,
That constantly weaves in
And out of our lives,
Like a ribbon in the wind.

My Inner Indian!

When I was very young
All I really wanted
To be was an Indian.
My mother always read to me –
Stories of fairies and elves,
Of princesses and ogres, witches,
And brownies who did good deeds.
Poems, "Wynken, Blynken and Nod",
"The Gingham Dog and the Calico Cat,"
And "The Sugar Plum Tree."
Books, *Alice in Wonderland,*
The Little Colonel stories, and
The Five Little Peppers.
(I wonder if my grandchildren
Have ever heard of any of the
Old-fashioned stories and poems
Which were all magic to me.)

But, most of all, I loved
Longfellow's poem *Hiawatha.*
"By the shores of Gitche Gumee,
By the shining deep sea water,
Stood the wigwam of Nokomis..."
I hear my mother almost singing
Those magical words from
"The Childhood of Hiawatha."
I could see Hiawatha growing up
And learning Indian ways in
The woodlands of his youth.
I wanted to live in the woods,

To learn to talk with animals
And know their secrets.
I wanted to wear moccasins
And build a birch bark canoe!

One Christmas my brother got
A cowboy suit and hat and holsters,
But I, wonder of wonders,
Got a "real" Indian dress
With designs of tiny beads,
A fringe on the skirt,
And a headband with feathers!
I told my friends I was part Indian,
That my great grandmother
Was a real live Indian!
When it got back to my mother
She just said, "What stories you tell!"

Although I outgrew the dress,
The dream stayed with me
Throughout my childhood –
Sort of wishful thinking.
I always wanted to
Be close to nature.
Much of my childhood
I spent by myself, somewhat
Of a loner, climbing trees,
Making hideouts in the woods,
Walking in streams
To "cover my tracks."

That "Indian child" I was
Still lives on in the
Recesses of my memory.
Maybe that's why now, "grown up,"
I love walking in the woods
Or foraging by the ocean,
Why *Stalking the Wild Asparagus*
Is one of my favorite books,
Why I love picking wild blueberries
And grapes and making jam, or
Digging for clams and mussels.
Why I HAD to experiment with cooking
Slipper shells and making
Seaweed pudding and "Sumac-ade."

Of course, I realize,
As well as anyone, that
The life of an Indian was not
As idyllic as I had once believed,
But, even now, after
All these years have passed,
It appears that
My "inner Indian"
Is alive and well and
Living on Martha's Vineyard!

The Doll House

It wasn't a fancy doll house –
After all, it was the depression.
It was just a folding cardboard,
Separated into little rooms,
With a green cardboard "lawn,"
A swimming pool, painted blue.

I was only seven or eight,
But I made beds out of paper,
And a table, I remember.
The stove and other furniture
I drew on the cardboard floors.
It didn't really matter.

Paper dolls inhabited
That wonderful place, and
What grand times we had!
There were feasts of
Orange paper hot dogs on
Crayoned blue paper plates

And tea and make-believe
Cookies and cakes
With princesses and queens!
We had swimming parties,
And we had dinner, and we
Put the babies to bed at night.

When I was grown up
And had a daughter of my own
I bought her a real doll house
With miniature furniture,
Bedspreads and curtains, and
Tiny little dolls that just fit!

But the doll house gathered dust
On the table in her room,
I know now what was missing.
It was the fun of making it all up,
Of doing it yourself!
The fun of imagining !

Childhood 1935-1945

I've never really wished
To be a child again.
For growing up's too hard
To even put to pen.
But somehow, in my mind,
The difficulties fade.
The memories that linger
Are joys that childhood made.

The endless summer days
Making hideouts, climbing trees,
Spying on the neighbor boys,
Or hanging by my knees!
I breathe the stuffy August air,
Sit dreaming by a stream
That ripples over roots and stones
Between two banks of green.

When the days were really hot
Our bathing suits we wore
To squirt our friends with hoses
'Til Mother said, "No more!"
On other days we put on plays
And practiced grown-up looks
And acted out the characters
We'd read about in books

In spring we wore our roller skates
That clamped on shoes with keys.
We rumbled down the sidewalks
And often skinned our knees!
We went to church on Easter –
White gloves we'd surely use –
With brand-new suits or dresses,
Flowery hats and patent shoes!

Winter was a great time
For skating on the pond,
Our toes and fingers frozen,
But how we whirled around!
And now the scene has changed
To a hill that's thick with snow.
And now I'm flying on a sled
To see how fast I'll go!

I still recall the smell of
Bonfires smoky in the fall.
Then Halloween, Thanksgiving –
Such excitement I recall!
I'm happy where I am today.
I've taken what life brings,
But memories can take me back,
And nostalgia ever clings.

Destiny

Don't laugh at daydreams!
That childish doodle
Scribbled on the math paper,
That drawing on the essay,
Those eyes that look out
The window and see beyond the
Teacher's understanding
Might foretell the future!

Dreams are seeds that grow
And twine into a bridge that
Ideas cross, to become the hope
Of realities yet to come.
Who imagined man could fly?
Who guessed a magnitude
Of horsepower could be contained
Beneath a metal hood?

The great designer starts
With the rough and childish
Sketches of that daydreamer
Who sees a vision past today.
The child obsessed with nature's lore
Becomes the famous botanist
Who finds a cure, in nature's
Hidden secrets, for human ills.

Beware the feverish world
That fears dreams, afraid of change,

That blindly reaches out
To stifle those who break the mold!
Hold in your palm your seeds.
Plant them in the fertile soil of thought.
Water them, feed them.
Let them grow unfettered.

For this is our tomorrow.
Without dreams, ideas, hope,
There cannot be a future!
Shrug off the disbelievers!
Smile back at those who laugh,
Prisoners in their strait-jacket minds.
Spin your dreams far out, and weave a
Gossamer and steely bridge to destiny!

Regret

We were cousins and had grown up
Close friends, living not far apart.
When I was nine and he was eight,
(His sister and my brothers were younger)
We were going to get married
Some day and have ten children,
Ten dogs, ten cats, and ten horses.

We played on the park playground
(He broke his arm falling from a swing).
We climbed trees, played card games
And board games and soldiers, and
In summer our mothers and we
Cousins took the long trek by train
And boat to swim at Nantasket Beach

One day my father found a new job,
And we moved away, far from home
As we had always known it.
My cousins also moved away,
To another, farther place, so
For years we saw each other only
On holidays or special occasions.

Although we weren't strangers,
We were never really that close again.
We grew older, married new sweethearts,
And started families of our own.
Of course we always made promises
On Christmas cards, "We really MUST
Get our families together this year!"

But it seemed only funerals or weddings,
A 90th birthday, or a 50th anniversary
Would find us once again together,
Reminiscing about the "good old days"
When we were all children, and
We were oblivious, and time
Seemed to stretch ahead into infinity.

We have lived nearer to each other
In the last few decades, but days
And years have drifted by. Often we've
Put off visiting 'til "tomorrow."
Now we are grandparents, even great
Grandparents, we and our spouses
Suddenly surprised with health issues.

And so we wake to find tomorrow
Is not always a possible option!
Finally, next week, I WILL travel –
It's not so far – to visit with my cousin,
His sister passed on, wife in the hospital.
He is not well, and she will not,
He tells me, leave the hospital.

Why, as years go by, do we always
Assume an endless supply of time?
We toss off, "See you next week",
Or "We'll get together next summer!"
But can we ever be sure of that?
Forget the excuses! Do it now!
We most regret the things we didn't do!

CODA

We had finally made new plans to travel,
At last, to see my cousin Don
And, possibly, even his wife, Ginny.
We had bought the ferry tickets.
But the night before, a storm came up
And forced us to cancel our trip.

. . . . .

Tomorrow I will go to his funeral.

Leona

An old friend died today.
I lift my head and look back,
Down the long fabric of my past.
I remember us at a party –
We partied a lot in those
"Salad days" of our youth!

At one another's homes
Babies, bolstered with pillows,
Slept on upstairs beds.
Good-natured competitions
Produced late night buffets.
The 20-40 Club – surely we'd
Never be more than 40!

What skits we put on!
The picnics and treasure hunts,
Singing in Musical Arts
Concerts at Troy Music Hall,
New Year's Eve – a dinner-dance,
Then on 'til dawn and
Bacon and eggs
At the all night diner.

In later years we kept in touch –
Calls, Christmas cards, rare visits –
Time always dropped away,
And we were back there yet!
Even now I only see Leona young –
Smiling that wonderful smile
That would light a room –
And singing, always singing!

Me

The body people never see
Is the one I keep inside of me.
I know they see me getting old,
With hair no longer quite so gold,
Perhaps my back is not as straight.
Maybe they see I have to wait

And walk, not run, across the street
To see a friend I want to meet.
My face has wrinkles now, I know,
Some things have sagged a bit below,
But this is not the one I see.
Inside my mind, it isn't me!

When I'm not looking in the glass
I never feel the years have passed.
The inner me says I could run
Around the block, and, just for fun,
Ride my bike 'til twilight's calling –
Or climb a tree, no fear of falling!

My hands, of course, do not have spots
Or knuckles swollen into knots.
Instead, a youngish woman's form,
Not yet assailed by age's storm,
Is lithe and not yet bowed by years.
So here's to the inside me with cheers!

Calendar II

Boxes! Days blocked
Inside of weeks, blocked
Inside of months, blocked
Inside of years! Inky lines
Of print within the squares
Spool out, grasping,
Their sticky tentacles
Binding me, blinding me!
My life, stored in boxes.
My life, broken into
Little white pieces to fit in
Little white squares,
With numbers circled
And captive lines of print.

Can I ever recollect myself?
Breathe! Breathe! Escape!
Tear loose the strangling
Strings of numbers, words!
Kick at the boxes, and
Pick the loose corners.
Pull apart the squares, and
Weave the sides into a line
That unspools far out into
A future that's unknown.
Make it bend and wander,
Take me where it will!
It's MY life! Can I do it?
I know I CAN! But will I?

Climbing

Life is like climbing a tree.
When you are still small
You stand in the shade
Of the huge, tall tree
And look around,
Your only world the brown tree,
The green grass underfoot,
Maybe some dandelions,
And your house nearby.

Next year you try to climb the tree
And realize the crackled bark
Is rough and scrapes your arms.
Taller now, you look about.
You see further now –
Perhaps across the street –
And notice not only grass
And flowers, but other trees,
Other houses, cars, and people.

When you are old enough
To climb into the middle branches
Your vision widens again.
Now you can see over the fence
Where other children are playing.
You can see all the way
Down the busy street.
A neighborhood spreads out
Before your wondering eyes.

As your life continues,
Growing into maturity and
Beyond is like continuing to climb.
Each struggle to a higher branch
Is a victory, leading to a
Broader vision of your world.
IF you don't look back and fear
To make the next effort,
And push on to another level.

Certainly climbing trees means
Slips and scrapes sometimes,
Falls that take away your breath!
Well, life can be like that!
Sometimes you try desperately
To catch that higher branch
And fail! But life is like that!
Relationships and branches break.
A sudden storm shakes your world.

But each time you reach higher and
Pull yourself up, bruises and all,
You conquer yet another trial.
Don't let yourself grow dizzy!
Fight panic and doubts! Climb!
Look through the lacy leaves
Of the highest branches
And exult at how far you've come!
Yes! Life CAN be like that!

LETTERS TO A SOLDIER

A Trilogy

I. Songs of Love

Love walked with me
In the crisp fall air
In a shower of gold and red.
Love showed me the print
Of a doe's foot
And where she made her bed.

Love sat by me
And warmed my heart
Under winter's starry sky.
Love fitted my soul
With gossamer wings
And taught me how to fly.

Love rode with me
Through soft gray mist,
Through feathery palest green.
Love opened my heart
And looked within
Where no one had ever seen.

Love walked with me
And held my hand
On a breathless summer hill.
Love lay with me
In the soft green grass,
And time and the wind stood still.

The sun was hot
And the green grass sweet,
And the leaves whispered quiet above.
With cherishing words
And gentle hands
You taught me the songs of love.

II. Why?

Sometimes, at unexpected times,
The bittersweet memories flood back.
Those magic years when the
Days and nights were endless
And seemed to run seamlessly,
One into the other.
When life itself was today,
Only the present,
Never the past or future.
Only the moments we seized.

We drank them in greedily,
With abandon, spilling carelessly
As if we would always have enough!
Away from studies, we roamed
The hills and woods of West Point.
We climbed the redoubts and
The lichen-covered rocks under
Trees of another century
That leafed out to cover us,
Keeping close our secrets.

There was that small glade
Where we glimpsed a deer with fawns
And found Jack in the Pulpits
Blooming in a sea of ferns.
We made love on the bed
Of soft green moss by a little waterfall.
So little did we think then of the
World outside our love – the world
Where, in a far-off Asian country
A war would crush our dreams.

But, inexorably, the day came
When we both were graduated,
I from college, you from West Point.
And, after the celebrations
Were over, you had to go away
(We did not know it was forever)
To serve your nation –
Until the day you gave your life,
At barely twenty-two, in the
Desolate foothills of South Korea!

III. Last Letter

You had to go and leave me.
I wasn't ready
For the emptiness,
The open sky and vacant roads
And fields and fields and fields!
In the pathways of my mind
I see you waiting still,
With that crooked smile
And waiting, open arms.

Can you see the past?
Can you feel a sense of loss?
Can you remember the
Blackberry kisses,
Juice running down our chins,
While we crumpled up
With laughter in the sun-sweet grass?
That pale, featureless room with
The ugly flowered bedspread
Where we made love,
Cocooned in blankets, and
Fought away the dawn?
The frigid Catskills lake,
Buildings boarded for the winter,
Where we laughed and
Swam and ran out blue and shivering
To the old, green van, where,
Wrapped in clothes and quilt,
We warmed ourselves with coffee
From a thermos and
Ate ham sandwiches?

Now you are forever gone,
I feel my grief in silence –
No public rituals for me.
And so I add this last letter
To the small packet in
My hand and light the match.
The wind fans the flickering flame,
And my eyes tear up and sting
As smoke and flames and ashes swirl
Upward, then vanish in the wind.

Coda

Now I rage against the pain
Of all those who since have lost
Fathers, sons, brothers, sisters, lovers,
Against lives squandered, dreams shattered,
In frozen mountains of Afghanistan,
In muddy swamps of Vietnam,
In burning deserts of Iraq.
I wail in the darkness – "Listen!
Listen! Surely God by any name
Never created humankind to hate,
To kill, and do it in His name!"
But why does no one hear?

About the Author

BARBARA POPE PECKHAM lived in Massachusetts as a child, moved to Connecticut for grade school and lived in Hamden, Connecticut until she married. After her husband, Douglas, returned from Korea, they moved to Troy, New York, where they lived until he was transferred to Syracuse, New York. In 2001 they moved to Martha's Vineyard permanently to the old Victorian house in Oak Bluffs that they have owned since 1971.

EDUCATION: Two years at Vassar College. Returned to college when the children were young and attended Russell Sage College in Albany nights and, later, Syracuse University, from which she was graduated.

CAREER: Was Society and Woman's Page Editor for the New Haven, Connecticut *Journal-Courier* for three years. Worked for a public radio station and an advertising agency in Albany, writing radio and television commercials. After graduating from Syracuse, she taught in grade school for 24 years until retiring in 1990. Received Teacher of the Year Award from the Marcellus, NY, Rotary Club.

ACTIVITIES: Has always been active in her church and is in the choir at the Federated Church and chair of the Mission Committee. She was president of the Syracuse Vassar Club and was very active in the Syracuse League of Women Voters, serving on the board in many capacities. She is a past president of the League of Women Voters of Martha's Vineyard. She is secretary of the Community Solar Greenhouse in Oak Bluffs and an active volunteer there.

PERSONAL: She has two sons, Douglas, Jr. and Jonathan; and one daughter, Jennifer, all married and living in the Midwest. She enjoys cooking, preserving, gardening, reading, swimming in the summer, traveling, and her eight grandchildren.